MY FRIEND EDDIE

Nikki Saunders

Hey I'm Charlie, and this is my friend Eddie, he has autism.

Mrs Lines is good at helping Eddie and teaching us about kindness. Today we learned about how we are all different.

We all have different eye colour and hair colour, that we can see. Some differences we can't see, like food allergies, a headache or even our talents!

When I talk to Eddie, I remember to say his name first so that he knows I am speaking to him.

At playtime, we like to play stuck in the mud. At first, Eddie thought we would actually be stuck in the mud. We explained, "it's just a game".

Eddie will sometimes go off to play alone, that's okay, because he likes to have his quiet time.

Eddie doesn't like loud noises. Sometimes in assembly when everyone claps loudly, I pass him his ear defenders ready. He smiles, but doesn't always look at me.

Eddie and I met in reception class.
I didn't know what autism meant.
Eddie and Mrs Lines showed me some
books to help me learn about autism.

I love dinosaurs and Eddie loves cars. He knows **A LOT** about different cars and talks about them all the time.

Eddie is a good friend because he is kind, he is never mean to me. Sometimes he gets frustrated if he can't do something, but that's different. We like to search for bugs.

When Eddie gets really excited or frustrated, he can be quite loud and flap his hands. I will ask him if he is okay. Sometimes he will answer, sometimes he can't.

Mrs Lines said it's called, "regulating your emotions".

Eddie likes to repeat things sometimes.

3-2-1..

Eddie doesn't know how to ask to play my game.

So, he pushes or taps my arms sometimes, this is his way of saying, let's play IT again or the game we played before.

My teacher explains things to Eddie using clear short sentences. If you say long sentences, it can be too much for Eddie to listen to.

Sometimes Eddie says, "abort mission." This is from his favourite computer game. When he says this, it's his way of saying that he wants to leave a game.

There are things that Eddie can do in class, that I can't. But sometimes, there are times I can do things and others can't. These are called exceptions. If my teacher knows one of us has a problem, this is how she helps us with it.

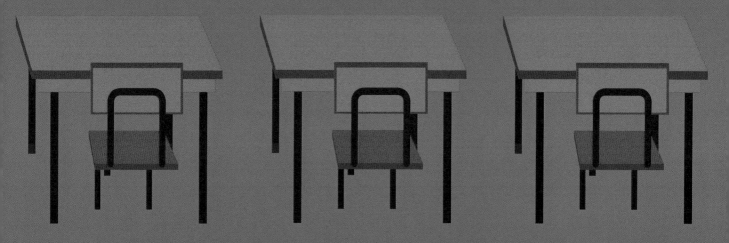

LEARNING ABOUT EXCEPTIONS

Eddie likes to line up toys sometimes, this keeps him calm.

Sometimes Eddie likes me to play his rules, this is because he can't ask me how to play my game. It's a lot for him to try and work out. His rules are easier for him. Sometimes I understand this. Other times, we play with different people. That's okay.

Sometimes Eddie says things that can hurt my feelings a bit. He doesn't mean to say these things and he doesn't know that some words are upsetting at times.

Eddie does say sorry to me. He is still learning and doesn't mean it.

In PE, we tried hula hooping! Eddie and I love doing this. He doesn't want to stop because he loves things that spin in circles. Our teacher lets Eddie play a little longer doing this.

ROUTINE

Now

Maths

Next

Playtime

Eddie likes routines and to know what is happening next. In class we have a now and next board.

WE ARE ALL DIFFERENT!

That's wonderful! Some differences are easy to see.
For example; different hair colour, eye colour, height
and skin colour.

Remember, always be kind and even people with autism are different from each other too.

We had a fire drill practice yesterday. Mrs Lines helps Eddie, as he can find it tricky to stop doing what he is doing.

Wow excellent timing today children!!

Eddie likes to cut out his favourite cars in lessons, he has lots in his tray already.

Eddie doesn't like to lose a scooter race. He gets really sad because he thinks he did something wrong. But his mum helps him on our way to school and reminds him it's okay, just have fun.

When we cross the road on the way to school.
I wait for my mum at the crossing. Eddie's mum can't
let Eddie do this, as he may just walk across.

We are all

Unique

and

Amazing!